PAUL ROMANUK

HOCKEY SUPERSTARS

2022-2023

Your complete guide to the 2022–2023 season,
featuring action photos of
your favorite players

SCHOLASTIC

TORONTO NEW YORK LONDON AUCKLAND SYDNEY
MEXICO CITY NEW DELHI HONG KONG BUENOS AIRES

THE TEAMS

CALGARY FLAMES
team colors: red, gold, black and white
home arena: Scotiabank Saddledome
mascot: Harvey the Hound
Stanley Cups won: 1

EDMONTON OILERS
team colors: white, royal blue and orange
home arena: Rogers Place
mascot: Hunter
Stanley Cups won: 5

ANAHEIM DUCKS
team colors: black, gold, orange and silver
home arena: Honda Center
mascot: Wild Wing
Stanley Cups won: 1

LOS ANGELES KINGS
team colors: white, black and silver
home arena: Crypto.com Arena
mascot: Bailey
Stanley Cups won: 2

SEATTLE KRAKEN
team colors: dark blue, medium blue, light blue and red
home arena: Climate Pledge Arena

VANCOUVER CANUCKS
team colors: blue, silver, green and white
home arena: Rogers Arena
mascot: Fin

SAN JOSE SHARKS
team colors: teal, black, orange and white
home arena: SAP Center at San Jose
mascot: S.J. Sharkie

VEGAS GOLDEN KNIGHTS
team colors: steel gray, gold, red and black
home arena: T-Mobile Arena
mascot: Chance

CHICAGO BLACKHAWKS
nickname: Hawks
team colors: red, black and white
home arena: United Center
mascot: Tommy Hawk
Stanley Cups won: 6

COLORADO AVALANCHE
nickname: Avs
team colors: burgundy, silver, black, blue and white
home arena: Pepsi Center
mascot: Bernie
Stanley Cups won: 3

DALLAS STARS
team colors: green, white, black and silver
home arena: American Airlines Center
mascot: Victor E. Green
Stanley Cups won: 1

NASHVILLE PREDATORS
nickname: Preds
team colors: dark blue, white and gold
home arena: Bridgestone Arena
mascot: Gnash

ARIZONA COYOTES
team colors: red, black and sand
home arena: Arizona State University
mascot: Howler

MINNESOTA WILD
team colors: red, green, gold, wheat and white
home arena: Xcel Energy Center
mascot: Nordy

WINNIPEG JETS
team colors: dark blue, blue, gray, silver, red and white
home arena: Canada Life Centre
mascot: Mick E. Moose

ST. LOUIS BLUES
team colors: blue, gold, dark blue and white
home arena: Enterprise Center
mascot: Louie
Stanley Cups won: 1

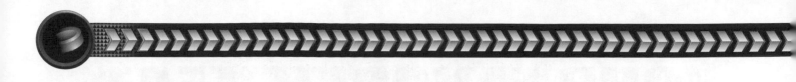

EASTERN CONFERENCE – ATLANTIC DIVISION

TORONTO MAPLE LEAFS
nickname: Leafs
team colors: blue and white
home arena: Scotiabank Arena
mascot: Carlton the Bear
Stanley Cups won: 11

. . . .

BUFFALO SABRES
team colors: navy blue, gold and silver
home arena: KeyBank Center
mascot: Sabretooth

. . . .

FLORIDA PANTHERS
nickname: Cats
team colors: red, navy blue and gold
home arena: BB&T Center
mascots: Stanley C. Panther and Viktor E. Ratt

OTTAWA SENATORS
nickname: Sens
team colors: black, red, gold and white
home arena: Canadian Tire Centre
mascot: Spartacat

. . . .

TAMPA BAY LIGHTNING
nickname: Bolts
team colors: blue, black and white
home arena: Amalie Arena
mascot: ThunderBug
Stanley Cups won: 3

MONTREAL CANADIENS
nickname: Habs
team colors: red, blue and white
home arena: Bell Centre
mascot: Youppi!
Stanley Cups won: 24

. . . .

DETROIT RED WINGS
nickname: Wings
team colors: red and white
home arena: Little Caesars Arena
mascot (unofficial): Al the Octopus
Stanley Cups won: 11

. . . .

BOSTON BRUINS
nickname: Bs
team colors: gold, black and white
home arena: TD Garden
mascot: Blades
Stanley Cups won: 6

EASTERN CONFERENCE – METROPOLITAN DIVISION

NEW YORK RANGERS
nickname: Blueshirts
team colors: blue, white and red
home arena: Madison Square Garden
Stanley Cups won: 4

. . . .

COLUMBUS BLUE JACKETS
nickname: Jackets
team colors: blue, red and silver
home arena: Nationwide Arena
mascot: Stinger

. . . .

WASHINGTON CAPITALS
nickname: Caps
team colors: red, navy blue and white
home arena: Capital One Arena
mascot: Slapshot
Stanley Cups won: 1

NEW YORK ISLANDERS
nickname: Isles
team colors: orange, blue and white
home arena: UBS Arena
mascot: Sparky the Dragon
Stanley Cups won: 4

. . . .

PITTSBURGH PENGUINS
nickname: Pens
team colors: black, gold and white
home arena: PPG Paints Arena
mascot: Iceburgh
Stanley Cups won: 5

PHILADELPHIA FLYERS
team colors: orange, white and black
home arena: Wells Fargo Center
mascot: Gritty
Stanley Cups won: 2

. . . .

NEW JERSEY DEVILS
team colors: red, black and white
home arena: Prudential Center
mascot: N.J. Devil
Stanley Cups won: 3

. . . .

CAROLINA HURRICANES
nickname: Canes
team colors: red, black, gray and white
home arena: PNC Arena
mascots: Stormy and Caroline
Stanley Cups won: 1

YOUR FAVORITE TEAM

Name of your favorite team: _____

Conference and division: _____

Players on your favorite team at the start of the season:

Number	Name	Position
_____	_____	_____
_____	_____	_____
_____	_____	_____
_____	_____	_____
_____	_____	_____
_____	_____	_____
_____	_____	_____
_____	_____	_____
_____	_____	_____
_____	_____	_____
_____	_____	_____
_____	_____	_____
_____	_____	_____

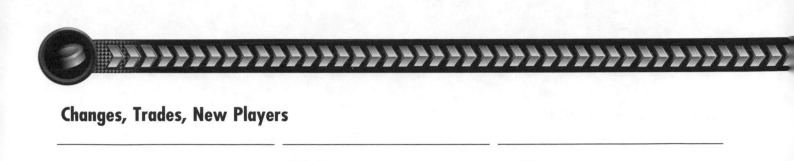

Changes, Trades, New Players

_____ _____ _____
_____ _____ _____
_____ _____ _____
_____ _____ _____
_____ _____ _____
_____ _____ _____
_____ _____ _____

End-of-Season Standings

Fill in the name of the team you think will finish in first place in each of the four NHL divisions.

WESTERN CONFERENCE

_____ **PACIFIC DIVISION**

_____ **CENTRAL DIVISION**

EASTERN CONFERENCE

ATLANTIC DIVISION _____

METROPOLITAN DIVISION _____

The Playoffs

Which two teams will meet in the Stanley Cup Final? Fill in their names below, then circle the team you think will win.

Eastern Conference Winner: _____

Western Conference Winner: _____

YOUR FAVORITE TEAM

Your Team — All Season Long

The standings of hockey teams are listed at NHL.com and on the sports pages of the newspaper all season long. The standings will show you which team is in first place, second place, etc., right down to last place.

Some of the abbreviations you'll become familiar with are: GP for games played; W for wins; L for losses; OT for overtime losses; PTS for points; A for assists; G for goals.

Check the standings on the same day of every month and copy down what they say about your team. By keeping track of your team this way you'll be able to see when it was playing well and when it wasn't.

	GP	W	L	OT	PTS
NOVEMBER 1					
DECEMBER 1					
JANUARY 1					
FEBRUARY 1					
MARCH 1					
APRIL 1					
MAY 1					

Final Standings

At the end of the season print the final record of your team below.

YOUR TEAM	GP	W	L	OT	PTS

Your Favorite Players' Scoring Records

While you're keeping track of your favorite team during the season, you can also follow the progress of your favorite players. Just fill in their point totals on the same day of every month.

player	nov 1	dec 1	jan 1	feb 1	mar 1	apr 1	may 1

Your Favorite Goaltenders' Records

You can keep track of your favorite goaltenders' averages during the season. Just fill in the information below.

GAA is the abbreviation for goals-against average. That's the average number of goals given up by a goaltender during a game over the course of the season.

goaltender	nov 1	dec 1	jan 1	feb 1	mar 1	apr 1	may 1

FREDERIK ANDERSEN

There was a sense of things coming full circle when goaltender Frederik Andersen signed a contract with the Carolina Hurricanes prior to the start of last season. Most fans associated Freddie with the Toronto Maple Leafs. Over his five seasons in the blue and white of Toronto Freddie played in 268 games, winning 149 of them. But it all came to a sad end when he became a free agent after the 2020–2021 season and the Leafs elected not to re-sign him. Freddie landed in Carolina for a fresh start. The interesting part? Carolina is the team that first drafted him back in 2010. He was drafted, again, by Anaheim two years later because he hadn't signed a deal with Carolina, but, technically, the Hurricanes were Freddie's first NHL team.

"It was interesting how things came full circle that way," said Freddie after signing with the Canes. "I'm just glad to have an opportunity to be here and play on a good team and do the best I can to help them win."

Freddie more than delivered on that promise. He was strong out of the gate, winning the first eight games he started, and nine of the first ten. He kept it going from there, helping the Canes to the highest point total in franchise history.

"We always had good goaltending, but Freddie has won us a lot of games," said Carolina head coach Rod Brind'Amour.

"Goalies, in general, we always get more of the credit than we deserve, and it goes the same way for the blame. It's just something that comes with the territory of being the goalie and it's just something you have to manage."

Part of Freddie's success comes down to his steady approach to the game. He doesn't get too caught up in the hype whether things are good or bad.

"You're going to have different emotional swings during a game," says Freddie. "It's a really exciting sport, so there's going to be ups and downs in every game and every period. The better you can ride that wave and not let it affect you, it's beneficial for you."

As much as Freddie enjoyed his time in Toronto, maybe signing with the Canes was the best thing that could have happened, bringing him back to the team that started his NHL journey.

DID YOU KNOW?

Freddie is a very good puck handler. He's so good that you'll see his name show up on the scoring summary some nights! Last season he led all NHL goalies with 4 assists. He's managed 13 during his career.

HOCKEY MEMORIES

Freddie has fond memories of his season with Frölunda in the Swedish Hockey League, in 2011–2012. He set a franchise record with eight shutouts and was off to North America the following season. "That was kind of where I was like, if I keep developing I can definitely have a chance to make it."

2021–2022 STATS

GP	W	L	OT	GAA	SO
52	35	14	3	2.17	4

Carolina Hurricanes' 8th choice, 187th overall, in 2010 NHL Entry Draft
Anaheim Ducks' 3rd choice, 87th overall, in 2012 NHL Entry Draft
1st NHL Team, Season: Anaheim Ducks, 2013–2014
Born: October 2, 1989, in Herning, Denmark
Position: Goaltender
Catches: Left
Height: 1.93 m (6'4")
Weight: 108 kg (238 lbs.)

KYLE CONNOR

WINNIPEG JETS

Last season was a very important one for Kyle Connor. Not only did he have the best season of his career, he won the Lady Byng Memorial Trophy as the NHL's most sportsmanlike player and was selected to play in the NHL All-Star Game for the first time in his career. Even more special was that he got a chance to share the ice with a couple of hockey buddies he's known since he was 10 years old. Kyle, Detroit Red Wings center Dylan Larkin and Columbus Blue Jackets defenseman Zach Werenski all grew up in Michigan and played together as they came up through the AAA ranks. Larkin and Werenski had taken part in the All-Star Weekend festivities before but it was a first for Kyle, and his hockey pals couldn't have been happier for him.

"He holds himself to a high standard," said Werenski about Kyle. "He brings out the best in other players . . . Obviously, the success he's having, he's earned it and he's worked hard for it."

It's been a journey. Kyle didn't just slide right into the NHL easily. He made the Jets coming out of training camp in 2016–2017, but he struggled to find his game at the NHL level. He looked lost on the ice at times and didn't have the offensive touch that he'd had in U.S. college hockey, and he was sent down at the end of November 2016 to play the rest of the season in the minors. He got a big chance early in the next season when he was called up as an injury replacement. Kyle found himself on the Jets' top line and picked up four points in five games. He was more confident, his defensive game was better, and since then, he's never looked back. He finished up that season with 57 points, led all rookies with 31 goals, and ended up finishing fourth in voting for the Calder Trophy as NHL Rookie of the Year.

> "I always want the puck, whether it's game-on-the-line or first shift. It's no different when the game ramps up. You just get more into it and want it even more."

It's come together nicely for Kyle. Jets' leading scorer, Lady Byng Trophy, his best season ever and an All-Star Game. Next year's plan? Some team success for the Jets!

DID YOU KNOW?

In Kyle's one and only season of U.S. college hockey, at University of Michigan, he led the NCAA in goals (35) and points (71) and was named USA Hockey College Player of the Year.

HOCKEY MEMORIES

Like many future NHLers, Kyle spent many years in the family garage firing pucks, off a square of artificial ice, at a net set up at one end of the garage. He estimates that he fired "hundreds and hundreds" of pucks. "The garage was pretty much destroyed," he recalls.

2021–2022 STATS

GP	G	A	PTS
79	47	46	93

Winnipeg Jets' 1st choice, 17th overall, in 2015 NHL Entry Draft
1st NHL Team, Season: Winnipeg Jets, 2017–2018
Born: December 9, 1996, in Shelby Township, Michigan
Position: Left Wing
Shoots: Left
Height: 1.85 m (6'1")
Weight: 82.5 kg (182 lbs.)

Leon Draisaitl

If you were looking for a hint that Leon Draisaitl had a knack for scoring goals, it might have come in the 2010–2011 season when he scored 97 goals in 29 games for the Mannheim Under-16 team in Germany. He caught the attention of scouts and, a couple of seasons later, moved to North America to play in the Western Hockey League with the Prince Albert Raiders. By 2014 he was playing in the NHL with the Edmonton Oilers, where he continues to fill the net. Entering this season, Leon has scored 254 goals in 558 games. Last season he hit the 50-goal mark for the second time in his career, ending up with 55.

> **"It's what I dreamed of doing and it's always been my goal in life to go and play in the NHL and, obviously, to be able to do that is very special to me. It means a lot. My dream became reality."**

"I'm proud. I'm very happy about it, no question," said Leon after reaching 50 goals on April 3, 2022, in a game against Anaheim. "But it also shows how great my teammates are. They're the ones that put me in these situations, they're the ones that get me the puck at the right moments."

Fifty is a magic number for hockey players. Of the thousands who have played in the NHL, only 94 have scored 50 or more goals in a season, and only three current players have done it more than once: Alex Ovechkin, Steven Stamkos and Leon Draisaitl. That's some pretty exclusive company. And it gets even more exclusive — Leon also hit the 100-point mark last season. He is one of only 24 players in NHL history to record 50 goals and 100 points in a season, two or more times.

"It couldn't happen to a better guy," says long-time teammate Mike Smith. "He's a workhorse out there. He kind of drives the pace for us. Obviously, he's huge on the power play [Leon scored a team record 24 PPG]. He's a special player to play with and an even better guy."

Expect more big seasons from Leon. How could you not? The indications have been there right from the start.

DID YOU KNOW?

Leon scored the last-ever goal at the Oilers' long-time home, the Northlands Coliseum (also known as Rexall Place), on April 6, 2016, at 18:03 of the third period, against the Vancouver Canucks.

HOCKEY MEMORIES

Leon's father, Peter, was a professional hockey player, so the sport has always been a part of his life. "I feel like I was born with ice skates. I don't know the exact age, but I was very young the first time I ever put on skates."

2021–2022 STATS

GP	G	A	PTS
80	55	55	110

Edmonton Oilers' 1st choice, 3rd overall, in 2014 NHL Entry Draft
1st NHL Team, Season: Edmonton Oilers, 2014–2015
Born: October 27, 1995, in Cologne, Germany
Position: Center
Shoots: Left
Height: 1.88 m (6'2")
Weight: 94.5 kg (208 lbs.)

AARON EKBLAD

If Aaron Ekblad isn't the best defenseman in the NHL, he's definitely in any conversation. He's coming off his best offensive season yet, hitting a career high of 57 points. He managed to put those numbers up despite having spent the off-season rehabbing from the fractured left leg that ended his 2020–2021 season.

> "I guess if you're setting lofty goals, which is what you should be doing in the NHL, you want to be able to set high goals and hope for the best, and work to be the best."

"Last season, before he got hurt, I thought he was a Norris Trophy candidate," said Panthers former head coach Andrew Brunette early last season. "He's so good at both ends of the ice and I thought he got back up to that level pretty quickly. It says a lot about him and his drive not to just be a really good player — he wants to be a great player."

One thing great players tend to do is to knock away excuses. Not feeling well? That's not an excuse for a bad game. End of a long road trip? Doesn't matter. Aaron had that kind of attitude at the start of last season. He didn't want his recovery to be an excuse or a reason for lower expectations.

"Everyone always says, 'Especially with what you went through.' I didn't want to think of it that way," said Aaron. "I wanted to think about it more like just picking up where I left off the season before."

That attitude, a belief in himself and a hunger to be the best, is a big part of what makes Aaron the player he is. Sure, there have been a few ups and downs along the way, but he has ticked most of the boxes as his career has progressed. He was drafted first overall, he was the NHL Rookie of the Year and, now, he's the best defenseman on the Florida Panthers and one of the best in the league.

"When I was younger, my agent [Hall of Fame member Bobby Orr] spoke to a bunch of us about how passion should play a role in absolutely every part of your life," recalls Aaron. "That lesson is one of the things that I've kept close with me throughout my hockey career."

There are still many years, and no doubt many more triumphs, to come in Aaron's career. His passion for the sport and for being the best will see to that.

DID YOU KNOW?

Why the number 5 on his sweater? "Gotta be [NHL Hall of Fame defenseman and seven-time Norris Trophy winner] Nick Lidstrom. I grew up watching him play. The guy's amazing."

HOCKEY MEMORIES

He's had more than a few, but scoring his first NHL goal, on November 1, 2014, against Philadelphia, is still a memorable one for Aaron. "It was a pretty awesome moment for me, a real milestone moment that I was able to enjoy with my teammates. I'll remember it forever."

2021–2022 STATS

GP	G	A	PTS
61	15	42	57

Florida Panthers' 1st choice, 1st overall, in 2014 NHL Entry Draft
1st NHL Team, Season: Florida Panthers, 2014–2015
Born: February 7, 1996, in Windsor, Ontario
Position: Defense
Shoots: Right
Height: 1.93 m (6'4")
Weight: 97.5 kg (215 lbs.)

JOHNNY GAUDREAU

Johnny Gaudreau knew that he would become an unrestricted free agent at the end of the season. It can be a distracting situation, with a lot of pressure to play well. Most players respond by playing some of their best hockey. So it wasn't a huge surprise that Johnny came up with the best season of his career, with career highs in goals and assists, and was rewarded with a big contract from the Columbus Blue Jackets after the season.

But the improvement wasn't all about the offense. Johnny also became a much better defensive player. Players and coaches call it having a "200-foot game." This means that a player works hard all over the ice and not just in the offensive zone.

"Johnny is one of the best 200-foot players in the league right now," said Flames head coach Darryl Sutter. "There was a buy-in in terms of the whole package. That says a lot about him and the way he approached the season."

"I would say that a few years ago I was maybe cheating a little bit more to the offensive side of the game," said Johnny. "Personally, I think I've gotten a lot better with my 200-foot game."

> "He's a rock star. He looks like he's playing pond hockey with his buddies, a bunch of 13-year-old buddies, the way he plays the games. It's fun to watch. It's probably even more fun to be him and play that way."
> — former Calgary teammate Blake Coleman

It was with his improved defensive game that he was able to strengthen his offensive game. Johnny finished up as the Flames' top scorer. He was only the tenth player in franchise history to hit the 100-point mark — the last was Theo Fleury, in 1992–1993. Johnny averaged 1.40 points per game, a career best.

He continued his strong play in the post-season, leading the Flames with 14 points (3-11) in 12 games. Calgary looked poised for a run at the Stanley Cup, but were knocked off by their great rivals, the Edmonton Oilers, in a tough quarter-final series. If you thought Johnny had loads of motivation heading into last season, wait until you see him this season. He'll be all about getting one step closer to the Cup with the Blue Jackets.

DID YOU KNOW?
In 2014 Johnny won the Hobey Baker Award as the best player in Men's U.S. college hockey. He was only the third player from Boston College to win the prestigious award.

HOCKEY MEMORIES
Playing in Edmonton during the NHL's "bubble" of 2020 brought back memories of a tournament Johnny played there when he was 10. "You never forget those times, hanging around with your buddies, playing mini hockey in the hallways. That was a fun tournament to be part of."

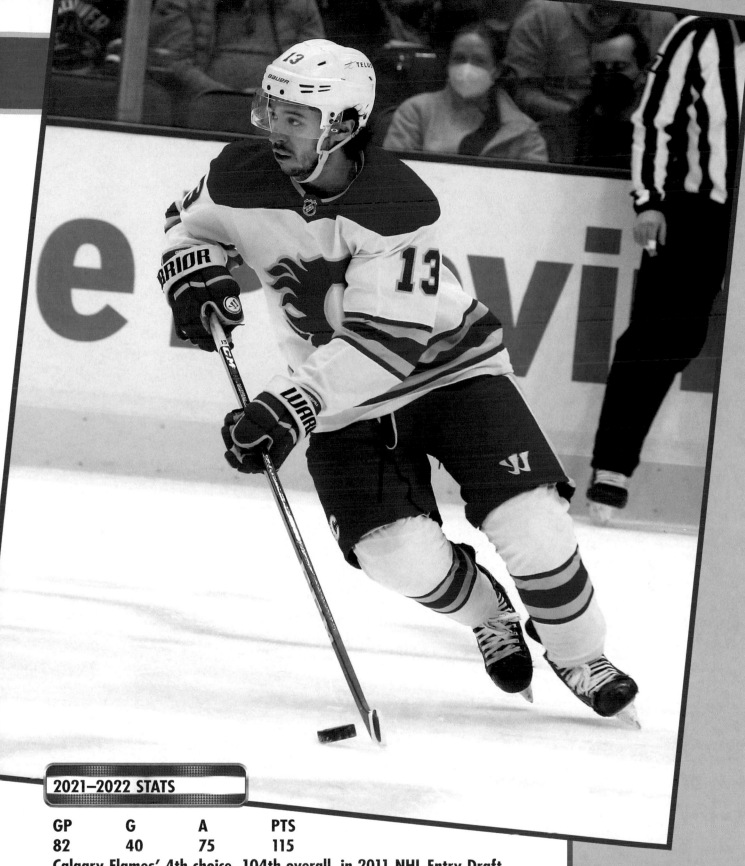

2021–2022 STATS

GP	G	A	PTS
82	40	75	115

Calgary Flames' 4th choice, 104th overall, in 2011 NHL Entry Draft
1st NHL Team, Season: Calgary Flames, 2014–2015
Born: August 13, 1993, in Salem, New Jersey
Position: Left Wing
Shoots: Left
Height: 1.75 m (5'9")
Weight: 75 kg (165 lbs.)

JONATHAN HUBERDEAU

There will definitely be some changes for Jonathan Huberdeau this season, but no doubt he'll continue to be one of the top, most consistent offensive players in the NHL. Jonathan has put up solid numbers since his first NHL game as a 19-year-old, when he scored his first goal on only his second shift. He won the Calder Trophy as the NHL's top rookie and hasn't missed a beat since. Last season was his best ever, with 115 points and the most assists in the NHL. What has changed is that, after 10 years in a Florida Panthers sweater, Jonathan will be wearing the colors of the Calgary Flames. He was dealt to the Flames in late July as part of a major trade that saw Calgary superstar Matthew Tkachuk head to the Panthers.

"I believe we've got an elite player in Huberdeau," said Calgary general manager Brad Treliving after making the blockbuster trade. "He was second in the league in scoring, he's been a top player throughout his career . . . He's one of the premier forwards in the league, not only what he does, but with the ability to make other players around him better."

Despite his terrific play, Jonathan didn't always get talked about when hockey fans discussed superstar players. One reason was that he had spent his entire career with a Panthers team that had struggled over many of those seasons. But those struggles started to turn to success and, with that, Jonathan started to show up on more hockey fans' radar. He'll have a chance to continue that climb with the Flames this season.

"I just love the game with a passion, and I don't try to put pressure on myself. I just like to play and try to be the best player I can."

Jonathan is in the prime of his career and it's a good bet that he will continue the same way he started his days in Florida — creating offense. Meanwhile, Flames fans are hoping that last season was the start of something that they'd love to see continue: some long-overdue success. Jonathan may be just the right player to nudge the Flames towards the ultimate goal — a Stanley Cup Championship.

DID YOU KNOW?

Jonathan left the Florida Panthers as the all-time franchise leader in points, with 613 (198-415). He will notch his 200th career goal shortly after the puck drops for 2022-2023.

HOCKEY MEMORIES

Apart from playing in the NHL, Jonathan's greatest hockey accomplishment was the 2010-2011 season in the QMJHL with the Saint John Sea Dogs. He led the Dogs to a Memorial Cup Championship and was named the MVP of the tournament.

2021–2022 STATS

GP	G	A	PTS
80	30	85	115

Florida Panthers' 1st choice, 3rd overall, in 2011 NHL Entry Draft
1st NHL Team, Season: Florida Panthers, 2012–2013
Born: June 4, 1993, in Saint-Jérôme, Quebec
Position: Left Wing
Shoots: Left
Height: 1.85 m (6'1")
Weight: 91.5 kg (202 lbs.)

ROMAN JOSI

The scouting report on Roman Josi, from pretty much the first time NHL scouts set eyes on him, was "ultra-competitive and always seems to have the puck on his stick."

Nashville assistant general manager and director of scouting Jeff Kealty recalled seeing Roman playing for Switzerland, against Canada, at the 2007 World Junior Championship.

"He had the puck all game and he had that ultra-competitiveness where you know he wanted to make a difference and was always up ice, looking to push things forward. He didn't take a back seat to anybody."

That competitive fire has made Roman one of the best defensemen in the game and the leader of the Nashville Predators. The Preds made sure that Roman would likely end his career in a Nashville sweater when they signed him to an eight-year contract extension in 2019. He responded by finishing up the season with a then-career-high 65 points (16-49) and winning the Norris Trophy as the top defenseman in the NHL.

"You sign a contract like that and you think to yourself that you now have to earn it and prove something; so it was very satisfying," said Roman of his big season.

Unfortunately for Roman, his game lost some of that sparkle the following season. Maybe it was the strange schedule in the NHL. Playing in the NHL bubble put many players off their regular routines. Whatever the case, Roman kicked it back into gear last season as he put up the best numbers of his career and finished second in voting for the Norris Trophy to Colorado's Cale Makar.

"I truly believe the best is yet to come. Just like one of his heroes, and another Swiss superstar athlete, Roger Federer, we have no doubt that Roman will get better with age."
— Nashville GM David Poile

"I tried to focus on the day-to-day instead of focusing on results," says Roman. "You need to have goals but you have to enjoy the whole process. You have to enjoy every day."

As Roman enters his 12th season in the NHL, he has become, without a doubt, the face of the Predators franchise. There would be no one more suitable to hoist Nashville's first Stanley Cup above his shoulders.

DID YOU KNOW?

Roman has scored more points in the NHL than any other Swiss-born player. Entering this season he has 542 career points. The next closest is retired defenseman Mark Streit, who finished up his career with 434.

HOCKEY MEMORIES

Roman was front and center for one of Switzerland's greatest hockey moments: a silver medal at the 2013 World Championship. He was named the top defenseman at the tournament. "That is one of my favorite hockey memories. Especially defeating the Americans 3-0 in the semifinal."

2021–2022 STATS

GP	G	A	PTS
80	23	73	96

Nashville Predators' 3rd choice, 38th overall, in 2008 NHL Entry Draft
1st NHL Team, Season: Nashville Predators, 2011–2012
Born: June 1, 1990, in Bern, Switzerland
Position: Defense
Shoots: Left
Height: 1.85 m (6'1")
Weight: 91 kg (201 lbs.)

Nazem Kadri

There is nothing like a little change to motivate a hockey player to work that extra little bit to be just a bit better. Take veteran forward Nazem Kadri as an example. The former first-round pick spent the first nine seasons of his career playing for the club that drafted him — the Toronto Maple Leafs. Nazem had some good seasons in Toronto, but an off-season trade prior to the start of the 2019–2020 season saw him land in Colorado. Nazem was motivated. He wanted to show the Leafs that they'd made a mistake trading him. During his time in Colorado he's done a pretty good job of that.

"When it happened it was a bit of a bitter situation," recalled Nazem. "But it ended up being bittersweet. I was put in a great situation in Colorado, coming in with a great group of guys. It turned out to be a blessing in disguise."

> "I never forget where I came from, never forget my roots, my hometown [London, Ontario], and people who have been in my corner from day one, and that's my family, and I love them so much."

Nazem never played better hockey than he did last season as he helped Colorado to a Stanley Cup Championship. Again, he had some motivation. At the end of the season he became an unrestricted free agent, free to sign with any team he wanted. Nazem had the best season of his career, setting career highs in assists and points.

There has always been one aspect of Nazem's game that has given him trouble: he can sometimes cross the line between being aggressive and tough to play against and being dirty. He's been suspended six times by the league for dangerous hits. It's something he works on.

"I play on the edge, I play intense and I play with passion and emotion. That's what a lot of people like about me," says Nazem.

Being on that edge is what has gotten Nazem to where he is: a 12-year veteran in the best hockey league in the world and a Stanley Cup champion.

DID YOU KNOW?

Nazem's grandparents moved to Canada from Lebanon in the late 1960s. Nazem was the first player of Middle Eastern descent that the Leafs had ever drafted.

HOCKEY MEMORIES

Nazem's earliest hockey memories are centered around the backyard rink. "My dad always built one when I was two or three years old. He'd be out there, trying to help us skate."

GP	G	A	PTS
71	28	59	87

Toronto Maple Leafs' 1st choice, 7th overall, in 2009 NHL Entry Draft
1st NHL Team, Season: Toronto Maple Leafs, 2010–2011
Born: October 6, 1990, in London, Ontario
Position: Center
Shoots: Left
Height: 1.83 m (6'0")
Weight: 87 kg (192 lbs.)

CALE MAKAR

If you can count on one thing about Stanley Cup champion, Norris Trophy and Conn Smythe Trophy winner Cale Makar's game, it is that it will continue to be praised and admired by teammates, opponents and hockey fans alike. Last season, only his third in the NHL, Cale was drawing comparisons to NHL Hall of Fame defenseman Paul Coffey — four-time Stanley Cup champion, three-time Norris Trophy winner and the second-highest-scoring defenseman in NHL history. And those comparisons were coming from none other than one of the greatest players in the history of the game, and one of Coffey's former teammates, Wayne Gretzky.

"When I watch him play," said Gretzky, "he, his game, reminds me of Paul Coffey."

Cale put his cards on the table pretty early in his NHL career. He was going to be a difference maker. He scored a goal in the first period of his first game: a playoff game against the Calgary Flames on April 15, 2019. He took a pass from Nathan MacKinnon and fired a wrist shot past Calgary goalie Mike Smith. In his first season, Cale set a franchise record for most points by a rookie defenseman (12-38-50) on the way to winning the Calder Trophy as the NHL's top rookie. More good things followed the next season — he finished second in balloting for the Norris Trophy — and then last season he stepped his game up another notch as he set a career high with 86 points. That total, recorded at the age of 23, is better than the career highs of Drew Doughty, P.K. Subban, Alex Pietrangelo or Shea Weber. In other words, better than some of the finest offensive defensemen of the era.

"He might be one of the best defensemen ever to play by the end of his career, at this rate," said teammate Nathan MacKinnon.

"There's nothing better than this. You dream of this. It feels so surreal. It feels like a video game right now."
— Cale after Colorado won the Cup

Cale still has a lot of hockey to play, so maybe it's best to hold off, for now, on the "best of all time" labels. However, there can be no doubt that he's established himself as one of the best right now.

DID YOU KNOW?

Cale is only the third player in NHL history to win the Norris Trophy and the Conn Smythe Trophy in the same season. Bobby Orr did it in 1970 and 1972 and Nicklas Lidstrom managed the feat in 2002.

HOCKEY MEMORIES

"My parents have a really cool picture of me when I was about two years old, when we went on a vacation to Hawaii. They have a picture of me on the beach with a little mini-stick. That was the first time they put a stick in my hand and, by their accounts, I was stick handling and stuff."

2021–2022 STATS

GP	G	A	PTS
77	28	58	86

Colorado Avalanche's 1st choice, 4th overall, in 2017 NHL Entry Draft
1st NHL Team, Season: Colorado Avalanche, 2019–2020
Born: October 30, 1998, in Calgary, Alberta
Position: Defense
Shoots: Right
Height: 1.80 m (5'11")
Weight: 85 kg (187 lbs.)

JACOB MARKSTRÖM

Jacob Markström has really come into his own the last couple of seasons with the Flames. Prior to that, he'd spent six seasons with the Vancouver Canucks. Jacob struggled with a lower-body injury his first couple of seasons in Vancouver, but once he was healthy, he settled nicely into the role of the Canucks' number-one goalie. But it has been in Calgary, where he signed as an unrestricted free agent in October of 2020, that Jacob has become great.

"It's everything. It's not one thing. It's experience, learning to push yourself every day. Working hard, getting stronger, getting better technically. It's all of the above."

"Backbone, MVP, best player on our team, whatever you want to say, it's been that way all year," said Calgary forward Matthew Tkachuk after a game last season.

Check out these numbers: 37 wins, a career best. Save percentage (.922) and goals-against average (2.22), both his best since he became a number-one goalie in the NHL. On top of that, Jacob set a career best with 9 shutouts.

A few things contributed to that great season. One was his confidence level. If you're fortunate enough to stick around for more than a few years as an NHL goalie, your confidence increases, and one of the things that increases it is playing a lot. Your coach sends you out, night after night, and has faith in you even after the occasional rough start. Jacob started 63 games last season, more than he'd ever started in the NHL.

"You wake up and you've got to do everything right. It's an exciting time," said Jacob when asked about his heavy workload down the final stretch of last season. "This is where the fun hockey starts. You start playing for playoff spots and where you're going to end up."

Jacob was a big part of the Flames success last season — their best since 2018–2019, even with the second-round playoff loss to Edmonton — and they look to be even better this season. He's arrived as an elite NHL goalie. The timing for both Jacob and the Flames is perfect.

DID YOU KNOW?

Calling it "one of the first real-life decisions I had to make," Jacob decided when he was 14 to focus on hockey instead of soccer. It was a tough decision. His brother was already a pro soccer goalie and his dad was a soccer goalie coach.

HOCKEY MEMORIES

As a young man, Jacob made his way from Sweden to Ottawa for the 2008 NHL Entry Draft. He was taken as the first player in the second round by the Florida Panthers. "A great experience. It was fantastic. That's a memory, for sure, that I will keep with me."

GP	W	L	OT	GAA	SO
63	37	15	9	2.22	9

Florida Panthers' 1st choice, 31st overall, in 2008 NHL Entry Draft

1st NHL Team, Season: Florida Panthers, 2012–2013

Born: January 31, 1990, in Gävle, Sweden

Position: Goaltender

Catches: Left

Height: 1.98 m (6'6")

Weight: 93.5 kg (206 lbs.)

TORONTO MAPLE LEAFS

The Toronto Maple Leafs are one of the oldest franchises in the NHL: they were founded in 1917. But no Leafs player has found the back of the net more in one season than Auston Matthews did in 2021–2022. Auston scored 60 goals and took home his second consecutive Rocket Richard Trophy as the NHL's leading goal scorer.

> "There's no limit to his ceiling — because he's so good and he's so big and strong and fast and he's got a great release."
> — Wayne Gretzky

That was the least of it in terms of individual awards for the Leafs superstar. He was also named the winner of the Hart Trophy as the NHL MVP and the Ted Lindsay Award as the MVP as voted on by his fellow players.

"It's nice. I can't lie. It feels really good. It's special to have my family here with me," said Auston at the awards ceremony. "There are a lot of great players in the room, a lot of really deserving guys. This is definitely pretty special."

The accomplishments came fast and furious last season. He scored 50 goals for the first time in his NHL career, becoming only the fourth Leafs player to do so. Auston scored number 50 into an empty net against the Winnipeg Jets on March 31, 2022. He probably wished it could have been a little more memorable, but the fans in the jam-packed Scotiabank Arena didn't seem to mind. They came to watch a milestone for a man who is already being called one of the greatest players in Leafs history.

What would make Matthews the greatest? For many fans, it would be hoisting the Stanley Cup above his head. Despite another frustrating first-round playoff loss last season, with Auston playing the way he is, it feels like the Leafs are closer to that moment than they've been in a long time.

"I've been watching for so long," reflected Auston at the NHL Awards. "Six, seven years now . . . I think everyone knows, understands and realizes how hard it is. You need a lot of things to go your way."

DID YOU KNOW?

Aside from leading the NHL in goals last season, Auston also led the league in shots on goal. He fired a massive 348 shots on goal and scored on 17.2 percent of them.

HOCKEY MEMORIES

It was the NHL's 100th anniversary season, and the Leafs were hosting the Detroit Red Wings in an outdoor game in Toronto on January 1, 2017, in front of over 40,000 people. Guess who scored the winner in overtime? "It was definitely one of the best moments in hockey I've ever experienced. It was pretty special."

2021–2022 STATS

GP	G	A	PTS
73	60	46	106

Toronto Maple Leafs' 1st choice, 1st overall, in 2016 NHL Entry Draft
1st NHL Team, Season: Toronto Maple Leafs, 2016–2017
Born: September 17, 1997, in San Ramon, California
Position: Center
Shoots: Left
Height: 1.90 m (6'3")
Weight: 93 kg (205 lbs.)

EDMONTON OILERS

Last season was another amazing one for a man most consider to be the best player in the game. Connor McDavid won the league scoring title for the fourth time in his career and set career highs in goals, assists and points. He's a hockey hero to many. When Connor was a boy, his own hockey hero was NHL superstar Sidney Crosby. After injuries caused Connor to miss a couple of chances to actually play against his boyhood hero early in his career, he finally faced off against Crosby in his sophomore season. They met on the opening draw, and Crosby snapped it back before Connor had a chance to touch the puck.

"If you look at Bobby Orr, Mario Lemieux, Gordie Howe, Mark Messier, they got better every game, and the bigger the game, the better they played. They wanted that responsibility. And that's what Connor's got right now."
— **Wayne Gretzky**

Move forward another six seasons and, between injuries and the COVID pandemic, two of the greatest players in the game hadn't gone head-to-head in 760 days!

Connor and Crosby finally met up on December 1, 2021, in Edmonton.

"When you see the level he has been playing at," said Crosby, "it's hard to think that he can find another level. But I think that he's done that. That's maybe the most impressive part about his game this season."

Crosby also has loads of admiration for the way Connor has handled the expectations from fans and teammates. As with Connor, that responsibility has been there for Crosby almost since he started playing the game. It has most definitely been there for both players since their skates first touched the ice in an NHL arena.

"It comes with the territory and it's something that you understand and that you try to embrace," says Crosby. "That's something that he faces wherever he goes."

And that pressure, those expectations, will continue this season. Crosby played on his first Stanley Cup Championship team in his fourth NHL season. Connor is heading into his eighth. You want to talk about pressure?

DID YOU KNOW?

Connor was held pointless in the first two NHL games of his career. He finally scored his first NHL goal in his third game. He then went on a tear, picking up four goals and seven assists in his next 10 games!

HOCKEY MEMORIES

Connor's mother, Kelly, recalls her son asking one day if she could help him write a letter to Sidney Crosby. He wanted to ask him about the pressures of being a great hockey player. Connor was five years old at the time.

2021–2022 STATS

GP	G	A	PTS
80	44	79	123

Edmonton Oilers' 1st choice, 1st overall, in 2015 NHL Entry Draft
1st NHL Team, Season: Edmonton Oilers, 2015–2016
Born: January 13, 1997, in Richmond Hill, Ontario
Position: Center
Shoots: Left
Height: 1.85 m (6'1")
Weight: 87.5 kg (193 lbs.)

MIKKO RANTANEN

Once again, the Colorado Avalanche will head into this season as one of the favorites to win the Stanley Cup. Two seasons ago they finished tied with Vegas atop the league standings, and last season they had the best record in the Western Conference and finished up as Stanley Cup champions. The biggest reason for their success? Great young players they drafted and developed are coming into the prime of their careers. And right there on that list is Finnish superstar Mikko Rantanen. Despite missing some games, Mikko led the Avalanche in scoring with a career-best 36 goals and 92 points.

> "I don't set goals for myself at the start of a season. I don't think that's the way to go. Winning is the hardest part. If you do the right things on the ice, the points will come."

There are so many other great players on the Avalanche that Mikko sometimes gets lost in the shuffle. Gabriel Landeskog, Nathan MacKinnon and Cale Makar have all been playing great hockey the last couple of seasons, but there was no doubt that last season Mikko turned it up a notch.

"He has really come into his own," said Colorado head coach Jared Bednar. "Even nights when he's not quite feeling it or he's fighting things a little, he finds a way to make a play or two a game to get on the scoresheet. To be able to produce even when you're not at your best is hard to do. It takes special talent."

Mikko has also emerged as more of a leader the last couple of seasons. He's earned the respect of his teammates and his coaches with his steady play and professional attitude. He proudly wore an "A" on his sweater last season as a full-time alternate captain (he had filled in as an alternate captain the prior season when Erik Johnson was out with a concussion).

"It's a huge honor. This is a legendary organization, the history they have. I'm really proud of it," said Mikko.

It's an organization that appears ready to add to its great history by trying to win back-to-back championships. Mikko will be right there, playing an important role.

DID YOU KNOW?

Mikko recorded 20 assists during last season's playoffs. Eight of them came in the Final against Tampa, just one assist shy of tying the NHL record for assists in a Stanley Cup Final.

HOCKEY MEMORIES

Mikko was a big part of Finland's 2016 World Junior Championship win in Helsinki, the capital of his native country. "That was an unbelievable moment. When you win, you share that moment with the great guys on your team. It's an amazing feeling."

2021–2022 STATS

GP	G	A	PTS
75	36	56	92

Colorado Avalanche's 1st choice, 10th overall, in 2015 NHL Entry Draft
1st NHL Team, Season: Colorado Avalanche, 2016–2017
Born: October 29, 1996, in Nousiainen, Finland
Position: Right Wing
Shoots: Left
Height: 1.93 m (6'4")
Weight: 97.5 kg (215 lbs.)

LUCAS RAYMOND

It has been a tough run for Detroit fans the last few seasons. But there is plenty to be optimistic about heading into this season. Winger Lucas Raymond and defenseman Moritz Seider both put up fantastic rookie seasons in 2021–2022. Seider won the Calder Trophy as Rookie of the Year. Lucas and Seider also became fast friends off the ice.

> "I think I learn new things all the time throughout the process: how to manage your body, how to manage your mind and be fresh for every game. If it's maybe not there, I have to still find a way to compete and play hard. It's just a process, and you learn throughout the season."

"We knew a lot about each other as players [they both played in the Swedish Hockey League in 2020–2021], but we really didn't get to know one another until we met in Detroit," says Lucas. "Everything was new for both of us and it was good to have someone to talk to, not even about hockey all the time but just about life. It was really good to have."

Lucas caught the eye of many scouts during the 2019–2020 season, when, as a 17-year-old, he played 33 games with Frölunda HC in the top league in Sweden. Scouts liked his great hands, his quickness, and his attitude and work ethic. Lucas showed what he was capable of early last season. In just the sixth game of his career, on October 24, 2021, against the Chicago Blackhawks, Lucas racked up a hat trick and an assist to lead the team to a 6–3 win. He became only the third teenager in Red Wings history to record a four-point game. Franchise icons Gordie Howe and current Detroit general manager Steve Yzerman are the other two.

"That's tough to take in," said Lucas after the game. "Those are two of the greatest players in franchise history. I'm trying not to think about it that much. Just keep playing, working hard and trying to develop and execute as a team and as a person every day."

It has been a few years since the Red Wings troubled anyone in the playoffs, but with players like Lucas leading the way, it won't be long before they do. Things are starting to speed up once again in the Motor City.

DID YOU KNOW?

When Lucas and teammate Moritz Seider won back-to-back NHL Rookie of the Month honors last season, it was the first time since 2016–2017, when Toronto's Auston Matthews and Mitchell Marner managed the feat.

HOCKEY MEMORIES

"I played a lot of sports. I played hockey at first, then soccer. I was even into gymnastics for a while. Also, swimming. My brother was the same. We played a lot of different sports. I was very active, but it ended up being hockey."

2021–2022 STATS

GP	G	A	PTS
82	23	34	57

Detroit Red Wings' 1st choice, 4th overall, in 2020 NHL Entry Draft
1st NHL Team, Season: Detroit Red Wings, 2021–2022
Born: March 28, 2002, in Gothenburg, Sweden
Position: Right Wing
Shoots: Left
Height: 1.80 m (5'11")
Weight: 82.5 kg (182 lbs.)

STEVEN STAMKOS

Last season must have felt very, very good to Steven Stamkos. He didn't miss games and practices with nagging injuries. Instead of rehabbing an injury before the start of the season and just trying to get healthy, he actually had time to work on his conditioning and skills. Whether he was at center or on the wing, he looked better than ever. The results bore that out. He finished up setting career highs in assists and points as he led the Bolts in scoring. It was the first time in his spectacular 14-season career that Steven topped the 100-point mark.

"To be with the core bunch of guys that we've had, it's a special group and a very special place to play."

"I've had some tough injuries and had to battle through some tough times and missed some amazing opportunities," reflects Steven. "But I take pride in being able to recover from those injuries and come back and play at a high level. There were probably a lot of people who didn't expect me to be where I am this year after the way things went in the last couple of years. That was motivation for me to prove those people wrong."

That's exactly the kind of talk you'd expect to hear from your captain and leader — a role that Steven has held in Tampa since March of 2014, when he had the "C" stitched onto his sweater after captain Martin St. Louis, a mentor to Steven during their time together in Tampa, was traded.

"I can't believe it's been as long as it has since I was named captain. I've tried to be a combination of all of the guys I learned from, including Marty, who were great leaders during my first years in the league."

The Lightning took a great run at a third consecutive Stanley Cup title last season, pushing the eventual champion Colorado Avalanche to six games in the Final. In the end, as is often the case in the playoffs, Tampa was battered and bruised and ran out of steam.

"It's one of the tightest teams I've ever been a part of," said Steven after the final game. "You remember the teams that won, and there are groups that are remembered forever, but this group has to go right up there. Who says we're done?"

DID YOU KNOW?
Steven played his 900th game with Tampa on March 16, 2022. He is one of only three players in franchise history to play 900 or more games with the club.

HOCKEY MEMORIES
There is a photo in the Stamkos family archives of Steven with his parents and the Stanley Cup at center ice in Tampa, after the Lightning won their second consecutive Cup. "You dream about your kid doing that," said Steven's dad, Chris.

2021–2022 STATS

GP	G	A	PTS
81	42	64	106

Tampa Bay Lightning's 1st choice, 1st overall, in 2008 NHL Entry Draft
1st NHL Team, Season: Tampa Bay Lightning, 2008–2009
Born: February 7, 1990, in Markham, Ontario
Position: Center
Shoots: Right
Height: 1.85 m (6'1")
Weight: 87.5 kg (193 lbs.)

BRADY TKACHUK

Patience is definitely something that Ottawa Senators fans have needed lots of recently. Since they made it to the Eastern Conference Final in 2017, they have not qualified for the playoffs. They haven't even come close. But there is hope. Young players like Tim Stützle and Josh Norris are developing nicely. Sens fans are also excited about their charismatic young captain, Brady Tkachuk. Last season, Brady put up the best numbers of his career as he led the team in scoring for the third straight season. It was a great way to cap off a year that started with signing a seven-year contract with the Senators and then, in November, being selected as the youngest captain in team history.

> **"We think that Brady's play, demeanor, leadership, is something that can help this franchise going forward and put us on the map. It puts a face to the franchise and you know what you're building behind."**
> — Ottawa head coach D.J. Smith

"Everybody has an impact in that locker room," said Brady, "and everybody has an impact in our leadership and everybody leads in their own way whether it's on the ice, off the ice or as a person . . . and everyone is pushing in the right direction."

Brady grew up immersed in the game of hockey and the culture surrounding it. His older brother, Matthew, plays for the Florida Panthers. His sister, Taryn, is a successful U.S. college field hockey player. And of course, hockey fans know his dad, Keith, who played over 1200 games in the NHL from 1991 through 2010 and was one of the great leaders and power forwards of his era. Keith Tkachuk was a captain in Winnipeg and Phoenix.

"I definitely leaned on him a lot for advice, especially since the added responsibility of being a captain. He's been there before."

Brady is well aware of how tough times have been for the Sens over the last few seasons. He also knows that things are heading in the right direction and that he loves playing for the Ottawa fans.

"I think there's a lot of great players in our organization and it's just a matter of time before it becomes a winning organization," says Brady. "I think right now, from the top down, that's what everybody believes."

DID YOU KNOW?

Brady was born and grew up in the U.S., and his mom is from Winnipeg, so he is a dual citizen. But in the hockey world, Brady is 100 percent American, having represented the U.S.A. in the World U17, U18 and World Junior Championships.

HOCKEY MEMORIES

Brady has amazing memories of watching his dad play in the NHL. "When the team won, we'd get to go into the locker room after the game. We'd play mini-sticks while the players got ready. It was always great to meet the players."

2021–2022 STATS

GP	G	A	PTS
79	30	37	67

Ottawa Senators' 1st choice, 4th overall, in 2018 NHL Entry Draft
1st NHL Team, Season: Ottawa Senators, 2018–2019
Born: September 16, 1999, in Scottsdale, Arizona
Position: Left Wing
Shoots: Left
Height: 1.93 m (6'4")
Weight: 95.5 kg (211 lbs.)

OLYMPIC SUPER STARS

Every four years we get the opportunity to watch stars from around the world play in the Olympics. These were some of the outstanding players in Beijing in 2022.

Sakari Manninen

Hilary Knight

Harri Säteri

JURAJ SLAFKOVSKÝ (LW) — SLOVAKIA

As a 17-year-old, Juraj Slafkovský held his own against players 10 or 20 years older. He led the bronze-medal-winning Slovaks, and the entire men's tournament, with seven goals. He was named to the Olympic All-Star Team as well as voted the Most Valuable Player in the tournament.

SAKARI MANNINEN (C/LW) — FINLAND

The Finnish veteran Sakari Manninen was a big part of Finland's gold medal at the Games. He led the team in scoring with four goals and three assists in six games, including a goal in the semifinal game against Slovakia.

HILARY KNIGHT (RW) — USA

Hilary Knight put up her best numbers ever at an Olympic tournament in her fourth outing. She struck for six goals and four assists in seven games, including a goal in the championship game against Canada.

HARRI SÄTERI (G) — FINLAND

Harri Säteri started five games for the gold medalists, including the semifinal game where he picked up the shutout in the 2–0 victory over Slovakia. Harri is a seasoned international veteran, having now played in four World Championships and two World Junior Championships as well as the 2022 Olympics.

SARAH NURSE (F) — CANADA

Sarah Nurse was a dynamo for Canada, leading the team, and the tournament, with 18 points (5-13) in seven games to win her first Olympic gold medal. She was also named to the Olympic All-Star Team. Sarah comes from a family of athletes — her cousins are NHL star Darnell Nurse and Canadian basketball star Kia Nurse.

Marie-Philip Poulin

MARIE-PHILIP POULIN (C) — CANADA

An Olympic Games veteran, Canadian team captain Marie-Philip Poulin cemented her reputation as one of the greatest clutch players of all time by scoring the gold-medal-winning goal for Canada for the third time in her four Olympic appearances.

ADAM TAMBELLINI (C/LW) — CANADA

Adam Tambellini plays professionally in the Swedish Hockey League and was proud to be a key part of Canada's team at the Games. He led the team in scoring with three goals and four assists in five games. He is also the son of retired NHL veteran Steve Tambellini, who played for Canada in the 1988 Olympic Games.

Adam Tambellini

Anni Keisala

ANNI KEISALA (G) — FINLAND

Making her Olympic debut, Anni Keisala was a workhorse in goal for the Finns. She played in every single game in the tournament for Finland and helped to lead them to a bronze medal. Anni capped a great tournament with a shutout in the bronze-medal game against Switzerland.

Countdown to the Cup 2022–2023

EASTERN CONFERENCE

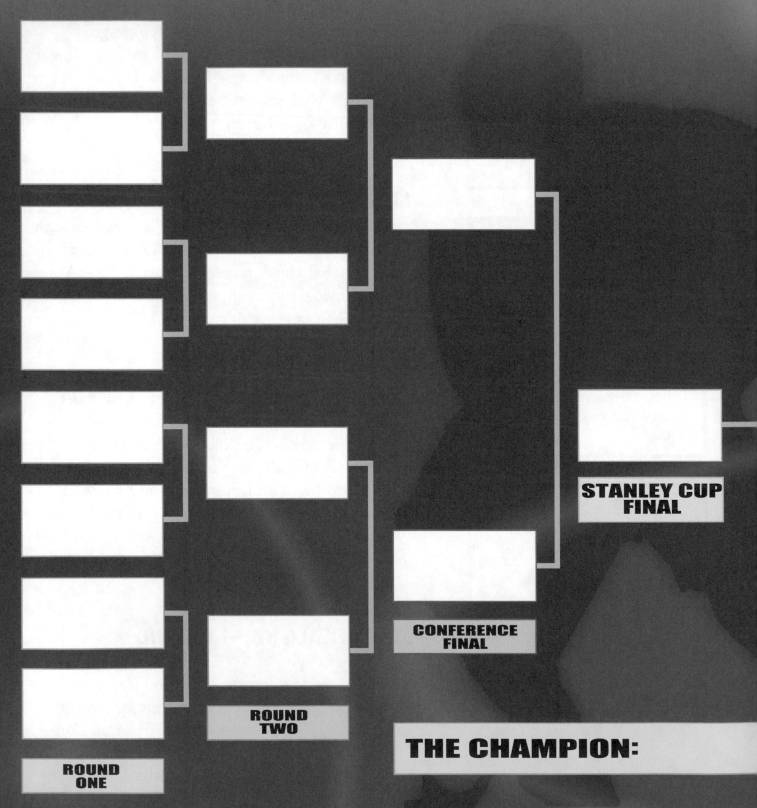

ROUND ONE

ROUND TWO

CONFERENCE FINAL

STANLEY CUP FINAL

THE CHAMPION:

WESTERN CONFERENCE

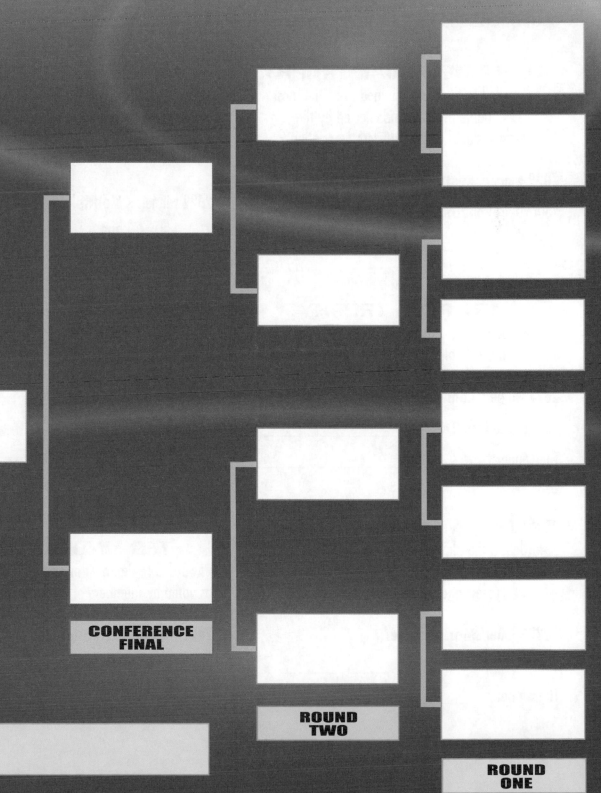

CONFERENCE FINAL

ROUND TWO

ROUND ONE

NHL AWARDS

Here are some of the major NHL awards for individual players. Fill in your selection for each award and then fill in the name of the actual winner of the trophy.

HART MEMORIAL TROPHY
Awarded to the player judged to be the most valuable to his team. Selected by the Professional Hockey Writers Association.

2022 winner: **Auston Matthews**

Your choice for 2023: _____

The winner: _____

JAMES NORRIS TROPHY
Awarded to the defense player who demonstrates throughout his season the greatest all-round ability. Selected by the Professional Hockey Writers Association.

2022 winner: **Cale Makar**

Your choice for 2023: _____

The winner: _____

ART ROSS TROPHY
Awarded to the player who leads the league in scoring points at the end of the regular season.

2022 winner: **Connor McDavid**

Your choice for 2023: _____

The winner: _____

VEZINA TROPHY
Awarded to the goalkeeper judged to be the best. Selected by the NHL general managers.

2022 winner: **Igor Shesterkin**

Your choice for 2023: _____

The winner: _____

CALDER MEMORIAL TROPHY
Awarded to the player selected as the most proficient in his first year of competition in the NHL. Selected by the Professional Hockey Writers Association.

2022 winner: **Moritz Seider**

Your choice for 2023: _____

The winner: _____

TED LINDSAY AWARD
Awarded to the most outstanding player in the NHL as voted by members of the NHL Players' Association.

2022 winner: **Auston Matthews**

Your choice for 2023: _____

The winner: _____

MAURICE RICHARD TROPHY

Awarded to the player who scores the highest number of regular-season goals.

2022 winner: **Auston Matthews**

Your choice for 2023: _____

The winner: _____

WILLIAM M. JENNINGS TROPHY

Awarded to the goalkeeper(s) who played a minimum of 25 games for the team with the fewest goals scored against it.

2022 winners: **Frederik Andersen and Antti Raanta**

Your choice for 2023: _____

The winner: _____

LADY BYNG MEMORIAL TROPHY

Awarded to the player judged to have exhibited the best sportsmanship combined with a high standard of playing ability. Selected by the Professional Hockey Writers Association.

2022 winner: **Kyle Connor**

Your choice for 2023: _____

The winner: _____

FRANK J. SELKE TROPHY

Awarded to the forward who best excels in the defensive aspects of the game. Selected by the Professional Hockey Writers Association.

2022 winner: **Patrice Bergeron**

Your choice for 2023: _____

The winner: _____

CONN SMYTHE TROPHY

Awarded to the player most valuable to his team in the Stanley Cup playoffs. Selected by the Professional Hockey Writers Association.

2022 winner: **Cale Makar**

Your choice for 2023: _____

The winner: _____

BILL MASTERTON MEMORIAL TROPHY

Awarded to the player who best exemplifies the qualities of perseverance, sportsmanship and dedication to hockey. Selected by the Professional Hockey Writers Association.

2022 winner: **Carey Price**

Your choice for 2023: _____

The winner: _____

REFEREE SIGNALS

Do you know what is happening when the referee stops play and makes a penalty call? If you don't, then you're missing an important part of the game. The referee can call different penalties that result in anything from playing a man short for two minutes to having a player kicked out of the game.

Here are some of the most common referee signals. Now you'll know what penalties are being called against your team.

Cross-checking
Striking an opponent with the stick, while both hands are on the stick and both arms are extended.

Boarding
Checking an opponent into the boards in a violent way.

Charging
Checking an opponent in a violent way as a result of skating or charging at him.

Elbowing
Checking an opponent with an elbow.

High-sticking
Striking an opponent with the stick, which is held above shoulder height.

Holding
Holding back an opponent
with the hands or arms.

Hooking
Using the blade of the stick
to hold back an opponent.

Interference
Holding back an
opponent who does not
have the puck in play.

Kneeing
Using a knee to hold
back an opponent.

Icing
Shooting the puck across
the opposing team's goal
line from one's own side
of the rink. Called only
if the opposing player
touches the puck first.

Misconduct
A ten-minute penalty — the
longest type called. Usually
for abuse of an official.

Roughing
Shoving or striking an opponent.

REFEREE SIGNALS

Slashing
Using the stick to strike an opponent.

Spearing
Poking an opponent with the blade of the stick.

Slow whistle
The official waits to blow his whistle because of a delayed offside or delayed penalty call. Done while the opposing team has control of the puck.

Tripping
Tripping an opponent with the stick, a hand or a foot.

Unsportsmanlike conduct
Showing poor sportsmanship toward an opponent. For example: biting, pulling hair, etc.

Wash-out
Goal not allowed.